The Way of the Meditator

Chantelle Ramshaw

Presentation by *BookLeaf Publishing*

Web: www.bookleafpub.com

E-mail: info@bookleafpub.com

ISBN: 978-93-95755-56-6

First edition 2022

May this book be dedicated to you, the reader, with plenty of sacred happenings upon your path.

The Way of the Meditator
(Part 1)

The observer looks outward from within,
Encasing contemplative thoughts behind the
body walls,
The eyes gaze daintily; Outlooking the form in
front.
Be it today, or tomorrow, the inner alter
welcomes all.
Nomadic wander guides the arrived meditator
among any journey encountered,
Or therein about to be witnessed.

The meditator witnesses themself being birthed
from their rightful place, the soul tribe.
He bows to the Tree of Life, pardoning passers,
save inherent knowledge.
A right of passage emerges, where realisations
of yesteryear opens up glimpses of the inner
solstice.
The shagged sweeps of pampas bolstering
specks of lumen, insulating the forest bed.
The meditator dreams latent lands unknown, yet
travelled, and yet to be travelled.
The disserted dust laden mill welcoming the
resolute in spirit.

A spectrum not usually sighted within the cracks
of casted driftwood.

It is to contend with ruminating nostalgic
sensations contained in the innermost road map,
the very highway of the life force.
Smitten and carefully proven scenes journey the
wayfaring mind.
Suspended thoughts confined therein meditative
chambers gradually lose traction, dissipating
away.
The auric gland acts out inevitably, postponing
then pulling forth tides onto barren terrain.

Remnants of the unconscious mind begin to
come forth in unexpected ways,
To the supposed folk onlooking they do not
reckon it centric to anything already on their
path,
Being unaccustomed, their senses hence deceive
them to be readily unconscious..
Substances limit by glance, lest both time and
space are extracted, enhanced.
Either extremity is conveyed to defuse non
truths out, to reveal itself.
It is through angled eyes and closed lids that
accesses closer, the inner gateway agape.
Then so meditator shifts Holy Sight onto
wherever alignment chooses the course.

With and through the parallel mind we harnessed
both dualities.
Simultaneously through the hemispheres we
activate momentum - two worlds co-exist,
collide.
It is without predestined expectancy or
familiarity, they are able to tread untouched.

Safe Place

Willowing embers trace evanescent skies,
Eyes glance slumberly with resounding swoons
of branched canopy,
Horizon sought ahead beholds paved fires,
Where neither a castaway hath ever known all
his days,
Aligning whom jaggedly cross unmarked road.
A haven recovered abiding the still,
Where here billowing empty a hammock,
Without a chord amongst the winds,
Neither distances between us it brings.

Offering

5

Here Thou submits earnestly an offering,
Not Plentiful it brings, yet as thine everything,
With palms resting towards the hyperion,
Where does lay in yonder meadow,
Find you a place burying the past,
Lest forgotten but forever grasped,
A scene to picture, a haven to stay,
These be the footprints on meditator way,
Nowhere here can it be born,
Lest eyes sleep before stretching the dawn.

Found

The seeker burrows tediously through past
wonderings,
Ploughing remnants to uncover the self,
Reminiscing livens forth a glimpse, a feeling,
The crumbs gathered of bypassed moments
promise irreverent sanctity,
Moulding the scene set of the everlasting
beginning,
Wasted recollections are neither optional, neither
with chained liberation,
With cupped hands it is fond of severance,
Within the cracks it surpasses exception,
Now Only whence consciousness had slipped,
It is then the search for I was found.

Hold Space

Synchronically the purified being fills their cup
day by day,
Filtering the mind and ridding it of maya.
These kind of happenings earned are through a
posture of the inner self,
Enlivened with suggestions beaming with prana.
Why does the obvious become apparent,
And all else disperses to the background, as if
non-existent?
The meditator is holding fast a selection
intentionally captured,
Pivoting from one scene unto the next.

The prostrated mind alleviates the load of space
occupied.
The reserved space is held for the reserved spirit.
The mindful atma reaches ecstasy in minute
moments of bliss,
Only shared in True Union.
The meditator breathes lifeforce not merely to
live,
Yet to retract and protract compelled power.
Each breath comes with deliberation an insight
on where it is directed.
Why does the soul traverse across the tides,

Only to reach the same subconscious shore?
This venture has become too vast a haven to
pitch their rugged tent.

They dwell verbally in the realm of the audible,
to where their ears tarry.
They seen not the transversal speech that has
rippled across all foreign and relative languages.
It is the invisible words, the non-discriminable
letters written in the telegram of yesterday into
the days ahead.
Each spoken gesture signs off with it a new verb,
A call to action that transfers over.
A kind of uncalled invitation is unknowingly
accepted.
The fewer associative harkenings, and the
further untrespassed trails into no mans land will
take us on a journey anew.

Where Did Your Learn This

Ones eyes decipher pierced feelings varying,
Where cyclical seasons rotate,
Only I see borrowed everythings,

Where had you learnt you had to please,
And chase another's totems with such ease?
Without advice and shared council,
No vessel, nor resource, only forced will,
Naively you wandered, unguided you searched,
Sheer nothingness plentifully emerged,
They protest by names surpassed in time,
Unheard of devotions to pilgrimage so wide,
Rostering through phases they unknowingly
convulse,
Yet you shall decide your Intuitive impulse.

Winding Avenues

I held in my hand a talisman of truth,
Wherever it went is wherever I'd go,
Be it day or night upon roads of silk,
Winding avenues lit by dimmed lampposts built,
I admired its lustre and glow that it made,
Retreating from here , a new world was paved,
Small precious stones caught my eyes,
Their striking beam made pebbles come alive.

Creation

Observing the moment gathers cohesion,
Where energy delves beyond all reason,
Every interaction creating founded life,
Conscious or not it's now within sight.
The power withheld has no bounds,
So unrimmed in its expanse it overflows,
Simultaneously giving breath to that reknowned.

The Seeker

Where the seeker fulfils their conquest, they have lost.

No more seeker, now they acquire with the next ambition... supplication unto the cause once chased.

They camp their rug atop the mountain, or therein pits indwelling the secrets of yesterday. Their venture is treaded light, in bare feet they walk the wild grasses. They sought themselves in a shared world, only to find themselves in all faces.

Revealed

The meditator conspires only that from within,
Deliberately they create fractures inside the
projections gathered,
Conspiring one day to breakthrough the latent
protection,
Until comes the day void ideals are no more,
When favoured principles become reluctantly
ignored,
Discarded are the now disposables,
And embodied are the qualities that prevail,
Gathered are the enrichments ancestoral scribes
tailed,
Our ancient selves knew what we reveal as
crumbs.
Tarried mantras from where we've come.

Purple Clouds

Upon the passing midnight hour,
Rests not the Watch Bird
Whom sits upon Severed Branch,
Whilst the Subtle Winds brush Delicate
Feathers,
Motionless He stalks the Passer-Byers,
From atop nestled presenting mist,
While the Purple Clouds conjoin,
And then arrives Golden Sky who peaks at those
whose Soul wishes to have a look.

Desert Ways

15

Wrestled ravens stalk ravage ways,
Where the cherokee once rest and tread,
Now rests bays of sands, amid in colours across
all the lands,
Whistling winds mirage the sound of waterfalls,
Yet all revealed is a dirt road after all,
Where it leads nobody knows,
Wherever man walks is where he goes.
Sweeping tides of orange earth,
The deserts ways inevitably diverts.

The Road to Answers

Confined amongst comfort,
You are cuddled in congestion,
To tarry away at the night hour stay,
And longing for liberation behind heavens gates,
Long you wait behind suspending prayers,
Hung on a rope of evidence seen,
And quickened it comes if you do believe,
Holdfast to it now, heavy is it's load,
Because once it's gone,
You'll be be back on the road.

Duality

Where can I find flat hills,
Yet form them amidst the mines,
Where can I walk the drenched desserts,
That quenches the thirst of the divine,
And too the clouded void,
That be not without loneliness,
A cape to cover the wounded,
A dressing for unveiling the unleashed.
Where there is a shelter is the covered,
Where is the presence is the absence of
nothingness.

Rest

Rest comes for those who do,
As a noun comes out from mouths of those
who've seen,
One creates pictures before they are to be,
And though it is not seen with eyes,
Rest comes for those who do.
I rest, I replay, I regain.

Naïveté Dreaming

There were times that knew no bounds,
As the naïveté skimmed through the foliage,
A paddock encrusted in sheen of the moon,
Beside a withered trinket fence beholding acres,
The young one trembled at sights so large,
Yet mesmerised they willing took the fall.
Through neverending lanes they counted the
coloured pebbles,
With eyes squinting, they bathe in sunlit
meadow.

Wilder

The wilderness in me stretches in the abyss of
the familiar,
The horizon line separating the shallows from
the expanse,
Where how far one goes too does the other,
No measure of light nor shade,
Can take away the nature of the one in infinite
motion.

The Way of the Meditator
(Part 2)

The meditator is not bound the pacing
impressions and stories devised.
They read the vibration, deciphers its effect and
as an alchemist,
Changes its entire meaning.
The subtle plane is receptive to all possibilities,
Yet forever passive as student unto teacher.
Vagabonds chase after such fields, as they forage
for dried shrubs dispersed across a marshland.
Liken to gloss stones polished by billowing
waves, they are struck by the notion of mere
difference.
What is sleeping still is awake,
And in a state of gathering, exercising the visual
apparatus of the precedential future.
Subliminally, one is what they believe, including
the unconsciousness.
The meditator has uncovered the enclosed
corners of limitation,
And steers towards deliberate digression.
The ebb and flow of the thought forms recur
continously,
Primarily where the meditator-student falls
weary, out of breath.

When one becomes wavering from centre,
The point of reference remains as is,
Yet the one hikes gradually off course.
Therefore it is with a firm grasp, and an aligned
structure can we skillfully choose where to
project our energy next.
The meditator dismisses what does not serve, the
gaze esteems itself to fall upon the wearer of the
sacred.
Wheresoever the crafted soul wanders, is the
abode of the Alpha.
The state of altered and embodied dhyana,
That which all concentration has followed like a
disciple follows the Master.
The meditator has pronounced their words via
the alternate route.
They have planted firmly the mindful ritual of
their own accord, bearing that whatsoever lead is
by the tongue in poetry, incited incessantly for a
lifetime.
Their recollections underived from senses,
But of the feelings magnetic.
The coincidental happenings appears in
moments fleeting,
Too swift to be sought.
Through caressing the mind's eye inward,
One reaches the communal sovereignty.
This ceremonial act has been the course long
worn,

The imagined dimension holding intact the
substance of all creation.
The trip taken along the dream trail wakens all
those who desire the same, they all land up in
the same destination despite opposing hills trod.
Along the journey, the mind has evoked
entanglements and devised a plan to guide
another way,
But the meditated mind re-directs the vehicle,
eliciting the true finding which were made for
this day.
Unequivocating belief, and self-ingrained
faithful dialogue has become the healing balm.
The meditator records their narrative in the
willowing dawn until the late hours of the night.
Each form rests next to the other,
The surface reads that space divides them.
The lowly vibrations process the objective world
on a scale,
Exposing their unconscious states.
Accumulating more space along the physical
planes,
Is deemed merit-worthy than those whom
occupies less.
One's auric field may bring in more than another
of the same substance,
Yet they do not resemble nothingness.

Peripheral eyes harken to capture what indwells the recesses of another's well.
It is the same haven as it were the postponed room of dreams.
It cannot be accessed by selective hearing.
Only can deciphered suggestions be understood in part.
The meditator inhales the present, yet was it not already residing inwardly?
Without speculation, by preceding events the meditator untethers their thoughts.
Their thoughts are suspended by their own beckoning of choice.
Associations in the imitational realm,
Or that unknown, are not to the assumed dispositions.
The meditator controls their repressed elements through repetition.
It is a kind of artificial detour, attempting to deviate attention.
The meditator leads their energy to flow in raging rivers, or be it still waters.
Imaginated reservations are their mantra, in temple within.
Offerings not of myrrh or incense are served, but the inner ashing wick of the dripping alter candle.

How many incitations? How long can the flame
be supported? The meditator's residence within
is luminated with everlasting supply.
It is where pondered concepts are residing, in the
womb of all creation.
One envisages discourses, yet the meditator
approaches the subjective like a consideration.

This way is wondersome to many,
And ascended upon by some.
The way was not a way infact,
It was already there.

The Ascendant

Devotionally the ascendant worships in the
willowed cave,
Mounted upon a distant hill,
Unknown yearns and pleas only heard by the
swallows,
They offer time in replacement of merit,
A priceless gift carrying no return.
They conceive of imaginary possibilities,
That eventuate from their steadfast ignorance.

Soulbound

Where pondering began was preceding
conception,
An inclination emerged to entity,
A thought embodied then takes form.
Shadows bow unto the Sun,
As a follower unto the master,
So too the soulbound body,
Whose days are numbered on the echos of the
strings of the lyre.

Stories Of Flutes & Bowls

Like the shivers along the spine,
Are the strokes of the flutes repercussions,
With a deep breathe ignites the quiver,
Like the reaching to collect incites the river,
Where does the hum finish its course,
After bypassing thine ears?
Singing Bowls gong layers present cells,
They reminisce and gather their stories to tell.